Dogsong

and Related Readings

McDougal Littell
A HOUGHTON MIFFLIN COMPANY

Evanston, Illinois • Boston • Dallas

Links to *The Language of Literature*

If you are using *Dogsong* in conjunction with *The Language of Literature,* please note that thematic connections can easily be made between the novel and the following units:

• Grade 6, Unit 2: The Need to Belong

• Grade 7, Unit 2: Life's Lessons

• Grade 8, Unit 2: Critical Adjustments

Acknowledgments

Page 8: Excerpt from book review by Stephanie Zvirin in *Booklist*, April 1, 1985. Copyright © 1985 by the American Library Association. Reprinted with permission of the American Library Association.

ISBN 0–395–78358–5

1234567—MAL—03 02 01 00 99 98 97

Table of Contents

Into the Literature: *Creating Context*

Through the Literature: *Developing Understanding*

Beyond the Literature: *Synthesizing Ideas*

Parts of the SourceBook

- **Table of Contents**
- **Overview Chart**
- **Summaries of the Literature**
- **Customizing Instruction**

Into the Literature:
CREATING CONTEXT

- **Cultural/Historical/Author Background**
- **Critic's Corner** Excerpts from literary criticism about *Dogsong*
- **Literary Concepts**
- **Motivating Activities**

Through the Literature:

DEVELOPING UNDERSTANDING

- **Discussion Starters** Questions for the class to respond to orally after reading each section, including a Literary Concept question and a Writing Prompt
- (FYI) **FYI Pages for Students** Reproducible masters that offer students background, vocabulary help, and connections to the modern world as they read the literature
- (FYI) **Glossary** Reproducible glossary of difficult words for student use from each section of *Dogsong*
- **Strategic Reading worksheets** Reproducible masters to help students keep track of the plot as they read (Literal and inferential reading)
- **Literary Concept worksheets** Reproducible masters to help students understand the use of literary elements such as theme (Critical reading)
- **Vocabulary worksheet** Reproducible master to help students learn essential vocabulary used in the novel

Beyond the Literature:

SYNTHESIZING IDEAS

- **Culminating Writing Assignments** Exploratory, research, and literary analysis topics for writing, covering both the main work and the related readings
- **Multimodal Activities** Suggestions for short-term projects; some are cross-curricular.
- **Cross-Curricular Projects** Suggestions for long-term, cross-curricular, cooperative learning projects
- **Suggestions for Assessment**
- **Test, Answer Key** Essay and short-answer test on *Dogsong* and related readings, and answer key
- **Additional Resources** Additional readings for students (coded by difficulty level) and teachers, as well as bibliographic information about commercially available technology

Overview Chart

Literature Connections	SourceBook	Reproducible Pages
Dogsong	Customizing Instruction, p. 5 Into the Literature: Creating Context, p. 6 Critic's Corner, pp. 8–9 Literary Concepts: Plot, Mood, Figurative Language, pp. 10–12 Motivating Activities, p. 13	**FYI, pp. 23–24** **Glossary, pp. 31–32** **Vocabulary, p. 39**
Dogsong Section 1, pp. 5–59	Discussion Starters, p. 14	**FYI, p. 25** **Glossary, p. 31** **Strategic Reading 1, p. 33** **Literary Concept 1, p. 36**
Dogsong Section 2, pp. 63–94	Discussion Starters, p. 15	**FYI, p. 26** **Glossary, p. 31** **Strategic Reading 2, p. 34** **Literary Concept 2, p. 37**
Dogsong Section 3, pp. 95–133	Discussion Starters, p. 16	**FYI, p. 27** **Glossary, p. 32** **Strategic Reading 3, p. 35** **Literary Concept 3, p. 38**
from *I Breathe a New Song*, p. 139	Discussion Starters, p. 17	
"Who Am I?" p. 143	Discussion Starters, p. 17	
"Susan Butcher" from *Champions*, p. 145	Discussion Starters, p. 18	**FYI, p. 28**
Words on a Page, p. 155	Discussion Starters, p. 18	
"The King of Mazy May," p. 182	Discussion Starters, p. 19	**FYI, p. 29**
"The First Americans," p. 193	Discussion Starters, p. 20	
"A Journey," p. 198	Discussion Starters, p. 21	
"A Mother's Yarn," p. 199	Discussion Starters, p. 21	**FYI, p. 30**
	Culminating Writing Assignments, p. 40 Multimodal Activities, p. 41 Cross-Curricular Projects, pp. 42–44 Suggestions for Assessment, p. 45 Test, Answer Key, pp. 46–50 Additional Resources, pp. 51–53	

Additional writing support for students can be found in the **Writing Coach**.

Summaries of the Literature

Dogsong
by Gary Paulsen

Dogsong is a rite-of-passage adventure told in three parts: "The Trance," "The Dreamrun," and "*Dogsong*." In "The Trance," a 14-year-old Eskimo youth prepares to escape the modern-day world and to embrace the old ways. Russel is aided in his quest by Oogruk, an old shaman of the village, who gives him a sled, dogs, and spiritual and practical guidance. In "The Dreamrun," Russel struggles to survive in the harsh Arctic region. His hunting experiences come to overlap with his "dreams" of a hunter from the Ice Age. The last part, "Dogsong," is a seven-stanza Eskimo poem in which Russel describes his trek.

RELATED READINGS

from **I Breathe a New Song**
selected by Richard Lewis
These three examples of Eskimo poetry describe the joys and pains of hunters from the past.

Who Am I?
by Patty Harjo
In her essay, the author poses a question that she answers proudly by examining the past, present, and future of her Native American people.

"Susan Butcher" from **Champions**
by Bill Littlefield
According to this biography of the record-holding Iditarod racer, the responsiveness of her sled dogs has proven to be the key to her success.

Words on a Page
by Keith Leckie
Lenore, the main character of this teleplay, shows promise as a writer and is chosen as a finalist in a competition. Tensions arise when it appears she is abandoning her Ojibway background.

The King of Mazy May
by Jack London
In this classic adventure story, 14-year-old Walt Masters must rely on a team of sled dogs in a life-or-death chase across the Yukon Territory.

The First Americans
by Marion Wood
This example of informational writing describes the forces that influenced the rugged way of life of first Eskimos in North America and the strength Eskimos derived from their religious beliefs and myths.

A Journey
by Nikki Giovanni
About to embark on a journey with a companion, the speaker faces the unknown openly and fearlessly.

A Mother's Yarn
by James Riordan
In this Arctic folk tale, young Nastai listens to her late mother's "voice" to overcome the hardships imposed by her father's sudden remarriage.

Customizing Instruction

Less Proficient Readers

- The vocabulary and poetic style of *Dogsong* present few, if any, stumbling blocks for less proficient readers. You might guide students into the novel by reading the first chapter aloud as a group.
- *Dogsong* has won critical praise for its faithfulness to the Inuit world view. To help students understand this world view, which may differ greatly from their own, present and discuss the **FYI** material (pages 23–27) before students begin reading.
- Use the novel's three section breaks as opportunities for students to make or confirm predictions about Russel's journey. Have students jot down their predictions and record the outcomes.
- In the novel's second section ("The Dreamrun"), Paulsen intentionally blurs distinctions between dreams and reality. The **Strategic Reading 1** worksheet can help students sort out events in this section.
- For students needing help with literal comprehension, reproduce and distribute **Strategic Reading 1–2** worksheets.
- Reproduce the **Glossary** (pages 31–32) for students to use as they read.

Students Acquiring English

- Introduce the term *coming of age* and invite students to discuss coming-of-age traditions in their cultures, including ceremonies (such as *quinceaños* parties, bar and bat mitzvahs, graduation celebrations) as well as the granting of new responsibilities and privileges. Have them note events that mark Russel's coming of age.
- Invite students to list and discuss domestic animals, such as the horse, water buffalo, camel, cow, and dog, that have played important roles in world cultures. Lead into a comparison of cultural attitudes toward animals. (Be aware that students from some Middle Eastern and African cultures may consider dogs unclean.) Encourage students to notice Inuit attitudes reflected in *Dogsong*.
- Have students locate Alaska on a map and share their knowledge of the area.
- If appropriate, use the suggestions for Less Proficient Readers listed above.

Gifted and Talented Students

- Discuss *Dogsong* as a *quest*—an adventure in search of something valuable. Note that quests include four key elements: a hero (either superhuman or ordinary and unassuming); helpers (supernatural beings, loyal friends, wise advisers, or animals); a dangerous journey; and a reward (a treasure, a useful object, new wisdom, or self-knowledge). Suggest that students make notebook entries to identify and keep track of these four elements as they read *Dogsong*.
- Have students record a quickwrite in their notebooks about their most unforgettable experiences with animals. As they read *Dogsong*, have them use their notebooks to chart Russel's animal encounters, comparing his experiences and outlook with their own.
- Have students read the **Critic's Corner** reviews (pages 8–9) and draw on material from the novel to support or refute one reviewer's opinion.

Dogsong

This tale of a modern Eskimo boy's vision quest reflects the author's vision quest as well. Gary Paulsen competed twice in the Iditarod, a grueling annual dogsled race across Alaska. He considers his years in the far north a pivotal part of his life. "I . . . changed, moved back in time, entered an altered state," says Paulsen. He explains, "I wrote *Dogsong* in camp while I was training for the Iditarod. It'd be twenty below, and there I'd sit by the fire writing longhand in my notebook. You know, I miss *Dogsong*. I wish I could keep writing it. It's like a friend who's gone away."

One inspiration for the novel came from a boy who ran up to Paulsen during a break in his first Iditarod in 1983. The boy hoped to learn from Paulsen how to work with sled dogs. Paulsen realized that traditional Eskimo ways were in danger of being lost, and he incorporates this theme into his novel.

Another source of inspiration was a mysterious figure who appeared twice to Paulsen in dreams during long, isolated sled runs. Both times, Paulsen's life was in danger, and both times, the dream figure brought Paulsen lifesaving ideas. Later, during an Iditarod stopover in an Eskimo village, Paulsen stayed at the home of an elder who resembled the dream figure. "Tell me now," said the man, "isn't this better? . . . With the dogs and the sled and the snow. . . . Come and live with us and leave that other way. It is no good."

Paulsen reflects, "It is an invitation that has never left me. . . ."

The Inuit of Alaska

Paulsen uses the term *Eskimo* when referring to native peoples of the Arctic; these people also call themselves *Inuit* and *Yuit*. The Inuit and the Yuit comprise two major groups living in the northernmost areas of Siberia, Alaska, Canada, and Greenland. Their languages and histories are separate but related. The groups include numerous subgroups, each with its own dialects and traditions. Throughout this SourceBook, the term *Inuit* is used, unless the former term is more appropriate to the context of a selection.

Alaska, where *Dogsong* is set, is home to nearly 35,000 Inuit—over one-third of the world's Inuit population. After the 1971 Alaska Native Claims Settlement Act, when the federal government returned 44 million acres of Alaskan land and over 900 million dollars to Alaska's Inuit and Native Americans, Inuit groups formed regional corporations to manage their land and investments.

Though the figures seem impressive, few of these corporations have yet begun to bring in profits. Most Alaskan Inuit live in government housing in small villages, supporting themselves as subsistence hunters, using motorboats and snowmobiles to net salmon and herring and to bag game birds, seals, caribou, and musk oxen. The young people, especially, feel the struggle to succeed in the world "outside" without losing their traditions.

Paulsen's Life

Outdoorsman Gary Paulsen has enjoyed over two decades of success as an author. His earlier years, however, were marked by hardship. Paulsen recalls his childhood as lonely and disjointed. He was born in Minneapolis, Minnesota, on May 17, 1939, as World War II gathered force over Europe. Seven years were to go by before he could meet his father, a career military officer caught up in the tumult of the war. Even after the war, the family moved too often for young Gary to feel that he belonged anywhere. "The longest time I spent in one school was about five months," he recalls.

Brighter spots in Paulsen's childhood were his grandmother and aunts, with whom he stayed periodically, and the library. Paulsen reflects, "[Librarians] didn't care if I looked right, wore the right clothes, dated the right girls, was popular at sports—none of those prejudices existed in the public library." Of his first library card, he has written, "I can't even describe how liberating it was. . . . It was as if I had been dying of thirst and the librarian had handed me a five-gallon bucket of water. I drank and drank."

Though Paulsen's young adult years were troubled, he managed to put himself through college and served in the Army, emerging as a field engineer. He found work in the fledgling aerospace industry. Before long, dissatisfied with his jobs, he began writing magazine articles and short stories. In 1966 his first book was published. By the late 1970s, Paulsen was penning several books a year, earning critical acclaim for young adult fiction and nonfiction.

Still, a successful writer is not always a financially well-off one. In 1979, Paulsen was living in Minnesota, supporting himself and his wife by hunting and trapping, when a friend gave him a team of sled dogs to make tending his traplines faster. Soon Paulsen was caught up in dogsledding and in the wilderness experiences it provided. Within a year he was working full time with his dogs, writing at campsites while the dogs rested during training runs. In 1983 and again in 1985 he competed in the Iditarod, an Alaskan dogsled race covering over 1,000 miles, from Anchorage to Nome. He thrived on the adventure, and so did his writing: in 1986 and again in 1988, he received Newbery Honor Book awards for his novels *Dogsong* and *Hatchet*.

Paulsen experienced a major life change when heart disease forced him to give up dogsledding. Wanting a clean break, he moved with his family to New Mexico and turned his energies to writing full time. Today, in good health again, Paulsen is a prolific author of works for adults as well as young people, winning consistent critical praise.

Critic's Corner

STEPHANIE ZVIRIN

Zvirin, Stephanie. *Booklist,* 1 April 1985.

. . . [R]eaders may find themselves drawn into Paulsen's latest novel about a young man's crossover into adulthood. Eskimo youth Russel Susskit is hard put to accept the modernity of the world in which he is growing up and mourns the loss of the old ways of his people and the songs that proclaimed their existence. Following the tutelage of a village elder, he embarks on a dogsled journey northward, a pilgrimage of learning, testing, and self-discovery, during which dreams of a different, long-ago self blend with reality as he struggles to sustain himself, his team, and the young pregnant woman whom he rescues. Paulsen's mystical tone and blunt prose style are well suited to the spare landscape of his story, and his depictions of Russel's icebound existence add both authenticity and color to a slick rendition of the vision-quest plot, which incorporates human tragedy as well as promise.

NEL WARD

**Ward, Nel. *Voice of Youth Advocates,*
December 1985.**

. . . While the language of the book is lyrical, Paulsen recognizes the reality of Russel's world—the dirty smoke and the stinking yellow fur of the bear. He also recognizes the reality of killing to save lives, and of dreaming to save sanity, in the communion between present and past, life and death, reality and imagination, in this majestic exploration into the Alaskan wilderness by a master author who knows his subject well. *Dogsong* is a novel of survival that can be read on many levels and by different age groups.

Critic's Corner

GEORGIA JOHNSON

Johnson, Georgia. *The New Advocate,* Spring 1995.

Russel is participating in the coming-of-age ritual of his people. . . . Paulsen . . . weaves or "folds". . . the dream world of ritual and ceremony into the character's reality of dogs, sled, snow, and landscape. In the dream state, Russel receives a vision of an ancient hunter who leaves his family and village to fulfill his role as a provider—to get meat for his people. The vision comes and goes in Russel's consciousness, and his awareness of time blurs between the present and the past. Ritual emerges as the organizing factor in this half of the story, and Russel is transformed from a boy to a man by reliving or reconnecting to . . . the song of his people.

Ironically, the Paulsen book is difficult for young readers because it captures the richness of ritual and the significance of a vision quest in integrating the individual into the ongoing traditions of the group. The struggle many readers have trying to "make sense" of *Dogsong* may be an indication of how aware the author is of his responsibilities as an outsider who writes about another culture.

ETHEL R. TWICHELL

Twichell, Ethel R. *The Horn Book Magazine,* July/August 1985.

The author neither romanticizes the hardships of this [Eskimo] existence nor exaggerates the peculiarities of its customs; yet he succeeds in giving the brutal North a poetry of its own. . . . [T]he merging of dream and real world is confusing from time to time, [but] Russel's mental and physical stamina are never in doubt. How he will survive his return to village life is left unanswered. It is enough to have followed him through a moving and beautifully portrayed rite of passage.

Literary Concept
PLOT

In *Dogsong*, a unique culture provides the backdrop against which a timeless plot unfolds. This **plot**—the connecting relationship among the main events in the novel—concerns the coming of age of Russel Susskit, an Alaskan Eskimo youth of modern times.

Most plots have a three-part structure. In the **exposition,** characters are introduced and conflicts appear. In the **climax,** the conflicts and action reach their most exciting point. In the **resolution,** an outcome is revealed or suggested, loose ends are tied up, and the story ends. Gary Paulsen divides *Dogsong* into three sections, roughly paralleling the three-part plot structure.

- The first section, "The Trance," functions as **exposition.** Here Paulsen introduces Russel and the shaman Oogruk. Russel's conflict appears as an unfocused feeling of discontent. The focus sharpens when Russel accepts the challenge of seeking a "song"—a traditional Eskimo way of understanding himself and his place in the world. The conflict gains an added dimension when Oogruk dies, leaving Russel with dogs, a dogsled, and handmade hunting weapons in the harsh Arctic winter.

- In the second section, "The Dreamrun," tension mounts. Russel begins learning how to balance his energies against the needs of his dog team and the demands of the unrelenting cold. Two more important characters are introduced: an Ice-Age man in Russel's dreams, and a pregnant girl, Nancy, whose path Russel crosses. The **climax** occurs when Russel, following the guidance of the dream character, kills a polar bear single-handedly and saves himself, Nancy, and the dogs from starvation.

- As "The Dreamrun" closes, the **resolution** begins. Nancy gives birth to a stillborn baby. Russel realizes that she needs medical help, and he plans a way to find it. He also realizes that his struggles have changed and deepened him and have in many ways linked him to Eskimos of the past. The resolution is capped by the novel's third section, "Dogsong," a chant in which Russel sums up his quest and the rewards it has brought him.

Presentation Suggestions You might use a diagram like the following one to let students visualize plot structure. Explain that the rising and falling line corresponds to rising and falling levels of tension or excitement in a story as the plot develops.

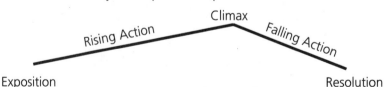

Be sure students understand that tension builds at a different rate in each story, so that the climax arrives earlier in some stories and later in others. Point out that exposition, climax, and resolution may vary in length and complexity, ranging from one sentence to many pages.

Literary Concept
M O O D

The many readers who find *Dogsong* "mystical," "haunting," or "compelling" are responding to Gary Paulsen's finely nuanced control of mood—the feeling that a literary work conveys to readers. Through subtle shifts in mood, Paulsen lets readers experience feelings of despair and hope, sorrow and exultation, exhaustion, wonder, and pride. Authors create mood through **diction**—word choice—especially the diction used in dialogue and descriptions. For example, a description of wind *wailing* or *howling* may suggest a mood of desperation, whereas a description of wind *whistling* or *singing* may suggest a more upbeat mood.

In *Dogsong*, changes in setting often correspond to changes in mood.

- The opening scenes of the novel, when Russel feels depressed, "in the dark," and spiritually impoverished, are set in the icy, dark Arctic winter, in the bleak confines of government housing in a poor village.

- Oogruk's home, where Russel gains a warmer sense of belonging and knowledge and a flicker of hope, is lit by the warm, golden, flickering light of a traditional seal-oil lamp.

- After Oogruk's death, Russel, in his loneliness and sorrow, heads northward, "into the mother of wind and the father of blue ice."

- Russel's time of greatest desperation and life-threatening danger comes during a howling Arctic blizzard.

- After the danger of death has been overcome, Russel, feeling renewed, begins the journey back to civilization to find help for Nancy. Simultaneously, the Arctic winter begins to wane and the daylight hours lengthen. As Russel and Nancy triumphantly approach the safety of the coast and civilization, the spring sun appears.

Presentation Suggestions You might have students make clusters focusing on the parts of *Dogsong* that affect them most strongly, including the feelings that these parts evoke in them. Explain that their responses result partly from their own unique personalities and histories, and partly from Paulsen's ability to convey **mood.** Present the literary definition of mood, and encourage students to describe the moods they notice at various points in *Dogsong*. If necessary, prompt with one or more of the examples listed above.

Literary Concept
FIGURATIVE
LANGUAGE

Dogsong reads like a ritual oration, reminiscent of a legend or a prose poem. This poetic quality results from Gary Paulsen's writing style. One hallmark of Paulsen's style is skill with **figurative language**—words used to express more than their dictionary meanings. Figurative expressions help readers picture ordinary things in new ways. In most of Paulsen's examples of figurative language, one thing is described in terms of another.

Paulsen is adept with three types of figurative language: similes, metaphors, and personification. Examples of all three occur throughout the novel; those that follow are taken from the climactic scenes in which Russel encounters and kills a polar bear.

- A **simile** is a comparison of two things that have some quality in common. A simile contains a word such as like or as to make an unusual comparison. For example, in *Dogsong*, Russel mentally tells the polar bear, ". . . the lance will enter you *like* light." (page 120)

- A **metaphor,** too, is a comparison of two things that have something in common. Unlike a simile, a metaphor does not contain the words *like* or *as;* it says that one thing *is* another. Paulsen writes, "The bear *was* a tower, a white-yellow tower. . . ." (page 119) Later, he writes, "The bear *was* a mountain of meat. . . ." (page 121)

- **Personification** is the giving of human qualities to something that is not human—for example, an animal, an object, or an idea. "'Cold is our friend,'" Russel tells Nancy. (page 113)

Presentation Suggestions You might present the definitions and examples of **figurative language, simile, metaphor,** and **personification** offered above. Then let students discover more examples on their own by scanning the first chapters of *Dogsong*. Suggest that students begin by locating similes, scanning for the words *like* and *as.* List their responses on the chalkboard and suggest that they list further examples of Paulsen's figurative language in their notebooks as they work through the novel. To help them grasp the evocative power of figurative language, you might invite them to use their favorite examples as inspirations for poems, quickwrites, or drawings.

Motivating Activities

1. **Picturing Opinions** In *Dogsong*, the deepening of Russel's insight is reflected in his attitude toward animals—including the sled dogs, for whose wisdom he gains respect, and the wild animals he must kill for food. Many students have strong feelings about animals and opinions about the ethical treatment of animals. Invite students to create drawings or collages that express their feelings and opinions. As they read, encourage them to explore effects that the novel has on their opinions.

2. **Linking to Today: Group Discussion** Lead a discussion in which students examine the increasing level of responsibility expected from them as they approach adulthood. Have students record their responses in their notebooks in the form of a *Then–Now* list of expectations. (Possible responses: *Then* students had few household chores; *Now* they have more or more difficult ones; *Then* parents told students repeatedly to do something; *Now* they must act without being told.) As students read *Dogsong*, encourage them to make a *Then–Now* list of expectations that show Russel's passage into adulthood.

3. **Brainstorming: Life in the Arctic** Have students brainstorm a list of things they would expect to see and do if they visited a North American Inuit family. Use the list as a springboard for discussing what students know or surmise about lifestyles of today's Inuit. Tell them to be alert, as they read *Dogsong*, for information that confirms or contradicts their ideas.

4. **Responding to Works of Art** Show photos of contemporary Inuit arts and crafts, such as ivory, bone, or soapstone carvings; pieced and embroidered anoraks, parkas, or mukluks; or drawings, paintings, or prints. (Articles in magazines such as *National Geographic, Smithsonian,* and *Natural History* are useful sources. As an alternative, show photos of traditional Inuit tools, crafts, and implements from museum collections.) Invite students to freewrite and discuss their impressions of the art. You might post the photos for students to return to as they read *Dogsong*.

5. **Tapping Prior Knowledge: Quickwrite** Invite each student to write quickly about the most difficult thing he or she has ever attempted. Encourage students to consider what happened, why and how it was difficult, whether they succeeded or failed, and how the experience has affected their views of themselves. As they read the novel, have them compare their challenges and their responses with Russel's.

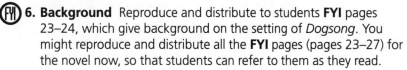

6. **Background** Reproduce and distribute to students **FYI** pages 23–24, which give background on the setting of *Dogsong*. You might reproduce and distribute all the **FYI** pages (pages 23–27) for the novel now, so that students can refer to them as they read.

You might want to distribute

(FYI) *pp. 23–25, Glossary, p. 31*

• *Strategic Reading 1, p. 33*

• *Literary Concept 1, p. 36*

Dogsong

SECTION 1

Chapters 1–5

AFTER READING

Discussion Starters

1. What is your reaction to Oogruk's final decision?

2. What advice would you give to Russel as he sets off alone on his journey?

3. In Chapter 3, after a first successful run with Oogruk's dog team, Russel suggests that he and Oogruk eat meat together to celebrate. Oogruk laughs and calls him "a true person." What do you think Oogruk means?

4. During another run with Oogruk's dogsled, Russel becomes stranded on an ice floe. What lessons do you think Russel learns from the run?

5. How would you compare the relationship between Russel and his father to the relationship between Russel and Oogruk?

6. Throughout Part 1 of *Dogsong*, Gary Paulsen begins each chapter with brief, real-life accounts of Eskimos who play no actual part in the novel's happenings. Why do you think he does this?

CONSIDER

✓ what Russel has in common with each man

✓ the advice each man gives to Russel

✓ what each provides for Russel

7. Of the things that Russel has learned so far, which do you consider most important? Explain.

8. **Making Connections** Oogruk tells Russel to set out with the dogs to find himself. In what ways do young people that you know attempt to find themselves?

Writing Prompt

Oogruk is a mentor—a wise person who gives valuable guidance to Russel. Write a **tribute,** an expression of gratitude, that Russel might write for Oogruk. Be sure to include the actions or qualities of Oogruk that Russel appreciates.

AFTER READING

Discussion Starters

SECTION 2
Chapters 6–10

1. Which part of Russel's dreams was most interesting or surprising to you? Explain.

2. What do you think is the connection between Russel and the hunter in his dreams?

3. At one campsite, Russel finds a carved stone lamp. Why do you think the lamp is important to him?

> ### CONSIDER
> ✓ where he has seen lamps like this before
> ✓ what he can use the lamp for
> ✓ how he feels after finding the lamp

4. As Russel considers all the details involved in dogsledding northward, he remembers what Oogruk once said: "It isn't the destination that counts. It is the journey." Evaluate how well you think Russel has followed Oogruk's advice so far.

5. **Literary Concept: Mood** At which point(s) in this section does the mood, or emotional atmosphere, seem strongest to you?

6. **Making Connections** In this section, Russel takes important steps toward independence. How do young people in your community learn about becoming more independent?

Writing Prompt

Russel can't decide whether or not to follow the snowmobile tracks he finds. Write a **dialogue** Russel might have had with himself, examining the pros and cons of his decision.

You might want to distribute

(FYI) *p. 27, Glossary p. 32*

• *Literary Concept 3, p. 35*

SECTION 3
Chapters 11—15

Discussion Starters

1. What effect does Russel's song have on you?

2. Of all the things Russel accomplishes in the novel, which ones impress you the most? Why?

3. How has Russel changed since the beginning of *Dogsong*?

CONSIDER

✓ his knowledge and skills

✓ his relationships with animals

✓ his relationships with other people

✓ his feelings about himself

4. In your opinion, will the things Russel has learned be useful when he returns to civilization? Why or why not?

5. Of himself and the dogs, Russel reflects, "We have fire between us that grows and grows. Fire that will take us north to safety, fire that will save Nancy." Explain what you think he means.

6. Do you think Russel and Nancy's friendship is equally important to both of them? Give reasons for your answer.

7. **Literary Concept: Plot** The **climax** is the turning point, the most exciting moment, in a story. Which moment do you think is the climax of *Dogsong*?

8. When you began this novel, you may have had very definite opinions about hunting and the use of animals for food. Explain how reading *Dogsong* has affected your views.

9. **Making Connections** Russel struggles to understand his heritage and to see how it fits into the modern world. In what ways do you or other young people share this struggle?

Writing Prompt

Imagine that members of Russel's village have gathered to welcome him back and to hear his song. Write an **introduction** for Russel that his father or another villager might make.

from I Breathe a New Song

Discussion Starters

1. Which one scene from these poems still lingers in your mind? Explain.
2. Which of the speaker's experiences in "Glorious It Is" do you think you would like to witness? Explain.
3. In "Signal Song on Capture of Polar Bear" the speaker just wants to mention, "for a moment and vaguely," that the speaker "overtook and fetched" a polar bear. How does this attitude compare with Russel's feelings when he shows Nancy the polar bear that he has killed?
4. In "Paddler's Song on Bad Hunting Weather," the speaker plans a song about a successful hunt, but the outcome is unsuccessful. What words would you use to describe the speaker?

Writing Prompt

In a quickwrite, write your **opinion** of the act of hunting. Be sure to give a reason or two for your opinion.

Who Am I?

Discussion Starters

1. Is the speaker's final answer to the question "Who am I?" one that you can appreciate? Explain why or why not.
2. Which part of the essay causes you to think of your own heritage? Explain.
3. This essay is one kind of answer to the question "Who am I?" In *Dogsong*, Russel Susskit's song is another. How would you compare Russel's song and Patty Harjo's essay?

Writing Prompt

Write a brief **character sketch** of Patty Harjo, using the information from her essay.

You might want to distribute

(FYI) *p. 28*

"Susan Butcher" from Champions

Discussion Starters

1. What are your impressions of Susan Butcher's life?
2. In your opinion, which of Butcher's character traits have helped her most in winning Iditarod races? Support your opinion with evidence from the biography.
3. In what ways does Butcher's adult life reflect the values she held as a young person? Explain.
4. In *Dogsong*, Oogruk says, "It isn't the destination that counts. It is the journey." How do you think Susan Butcher would respond to this statement?
5. How is the Iditarod race similar to or different from the journey Russel makes in *Dogsong*?

Writing Prompt

What would you like to know about Susan Butcher's life today? Write a few **interview questions.**

Words on a Page

Discussion Starters

1. What were your first thoughts as you finished reading this teleplay?
2. Would you have participated in the writing finals if you were Lenore? Why or why not?
3. Does Lenore's relationship with her father, Pete, strike you as a true-to-life portrayal of a relationship between a parent and a young adult? Use evidence from the teleplay to support your opinion.
4. What advice might Oogruk, of *Dogsong*, give to Pete about Lenore?

Writing Prompt

Write the **dialogue** for the conversation Lenore and her father might have while on a canoe ride following the District Writing Competition.

BEFORE READING

You might want to distribute

(FYI) *p. 29*

The King of Mazy May

Discussion Starters

1. Which scene from this story remains most vivid in your mind? Why?

2. Walt risks his life to help a neighbor. In your opinion, is the risk worth it? Explain your view.

3. Would you say that Walt "comes of age" in this story? Why or why not?

4. **Literary Concept: Figurative Language** In "The King of Mazy May," Jack London compares the rushing dogsleds to boats ("jumping and plunging and yawing like a boat before the wind") and to speeding locomotives ("The other sled was coming up like an express train."). Explain whether or not these comparisons help you picture the way the sleds move.

5. Compare the way Walt works with the claim jumpers' sled dogs with the way Russel works with Oogruk's dogs.

   ### CONSIDER

   ✓ how each boy communicates with the dogs

   ✓ when and why each uses a whip

   ✓ the attitudes each shows toward the dogs

   ✓ the results each gets from the dogs

7. In Walt's place, what do you think Russel Susskit might have done? Explain why you think as you do.

Writing Prompt

When the claim jumpers find Loren Hall's mine, Walt is alone with some big decisions—and he has to make them fast. Summarize what happens to him in a **cause-and-effect chart.**

The First Americans

Discussion Starters

1. In this selection, which information about traditional Eskimo life surprises you most?

2. Which description appeals to you more—the traditional life of the Eskimos or that of the Indians of the Northern Forests?

   CONSIDER

   ✓ what grew in the areas where each group lived

   ✓ their ways of getting food

   ✓ the kinds of shelters they built

   ✓ what they used to make clothing

3. Now that you have read this selection, do you agree or disagree that it is important to preserve traditional Eskimo and American Indian lifestyles? Explain why you think as you do.

4. "The First Americans" refers to "young men wishing to make their way in the world" who "sought . . . help [from the spirits] by going alone into remote and desolate places to fast and pray for guidance." How well do you think this description fits Russel's dogsled journey in *Dogsong*? Give a reason for your answer.

Writing Prompt

According to "The First Americans," a vision or dream could be an important source of ideas to early Eskimos and Native Americans. What purposes do you think dreams serve in American culture today? Write a **comparison** between the early view of dreams and what you think is the present view.

A Journey

Discussion Starters

1. Describe your mental image of the speaker in this poem.
2. Suggest some possible reasons that the speaker is not afraid, in spite of the uncertainties of the journey.
3. If you were to go on the journey this poem describes, would you like to have a companion or to be on your own? Give a reason for your answer.
4. **Making Connections** Which parts of this poem could apply to the journey you are making through life?

Writing Prompt

Imagine that the speaker has returned from the journey and wants to share details about it. Write a **feature article** that describes what actually happened.

You might want to distribute

 p. 30

A Mother's Yarn

Discussion Starters

1. Are you surprised at the way this story ends? Why or why not?
2. A twist of yarn left on the floor is the beginning of Nastai's prosperity. Do you think Nastai might have prospered even without the twist of yarn? Explain your answer.
3. Nastai hears her mother's advice in her mind, just as Russel Susskit, in *Dogsong*, mentally hears Oogruk's advice. Do you think either Nastai or Russel could have survived without the advice each receives? Explain.

Writing Prompt

Think of one valuable piece of advice that you could give Nastai or another character in the tale. Write an original **proverb** that sums up this advice.

These pages for the students give background, explain references, help with vocabulary words, and help students connect their own world with the world of *Dogsong.* You can reproduce these pages and allow students to read them before or while they read the works in *Literature Connections.*

Table of Contents

Dogsong

Naming Names

The word *Eskimo* comes from a Native American name for the Arctic natives. Today some continue to call themselves Eskimos. In their own languages, however, they divide themselves into two main groups—the Inuit and the Yuit (or Yupik). They add place names for further identification: Copper Eskimos, for example, from the Coppermine district of northern Canada; Polar Inuit, from northern Greenland; Nunivak Yuit, from Nunivak Island, Alaska.

Russel's Ride

Where does Russel live? His village is fictional, but Gary Paulsen may have modeled Russel's home on two real places: Shaktolik and Unalakleet, in northwestern Alaska. Both are Inuit villages on Norton Sound, an inlet of the Bering Sea. Paulsen has spent time with families in both. Russel's journey carries him northward from Norton Sound, across the Arctic Circle, toward the Arctic Ocean.

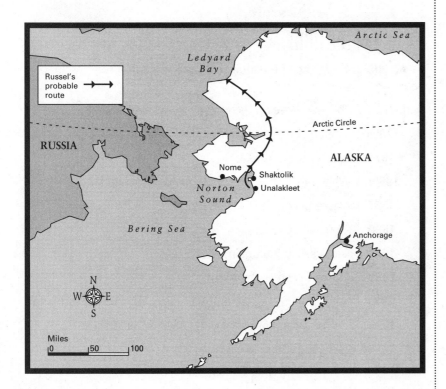

Chill Out !

If heat bothers you, you might try living in the Arctic. In northwestern Alaska, where *Dogsong* is set, temperatures do rise above freezing in July and August, but things stay predictably cool the rest of the year. Winter lows can drop to −40 °F, not counting the wind chill factor. Even in summer, the thaw extends only a foot or so into the ground. Below the surface, permafrost keeps the soil frozen year-round.

The Inuit …

- have lived near the Arctic Circle—in Siberia, Alaska, Canada, and Greenland—for thousands of years.

- are not Native American; their languages and culture are unique.

- are expert fishers and hunters in icy conditions that send most people packing.

- cope with winter months of solid darkness and summer months of solid light.

- enjoy their own games, including blanket tosses, face-making contests, and a complicated version of cat's cradle.

- have survived and thrived in one of the harshest climates on Earth, probably by sharing their food and shelter.

Dogsong (continued)

Village Life Today

Most modern Inuit groups live in the coastal villages of their ancestors. As in the past, they fish and hunt for most of their food, though they now use snowmobiles and motorboats instead of dogsleds and kayaks. Village schools teach English and Inupiaq or Yupik, the two main Inuit languages. Each village has a common hall where residents gather daily. Here they watch TV on the village set, swap news, use the telephone, order goods from "outside," or enjoy a sauna. Here, too, teens hold parties, and adults hold business meetings.

Regained Land

Banding together, the Inuit of Alaska sued the U.S. government for their lost land. In 1971, Congress agreed to return some of the land and to pay for land that could not be returned. The government set up companies to manage the land and invest the money, and the Inuit became shareholders. In the mid-1980s, profits began trickling in. True to their tradition of sharing, the Inuit have used the profits for the good of all, building local schools and medical centers, improving community halls, or bringing electricity to village homes.

Home Is Where the Frost Is

The Inuit traditionally lived in houses of rock and sod. Today villagers live in wooden houses. During the brief summer thaw, many Inuit move to fishing camps to net salmon and herring. There, where they traditionally slept in skin tents, they now have cabins or use standard camping gear.

What about igloos? Igloos have never been more than overnight shelters—but they're still used on some hunting trips. It takes only an hour or two to build an igloo, sawing blocks of ice or frozen snow, stacking them in a running coil, and packing the cracks with more snow.

History of the Inuit

40,000 years ago	Ancestors of the Inuit settle Alaskan coast
A.D. 1000	The Inuit develop technology for whale-hunting
1700s	Russian explorers and fishermen arrive in Alaska
1824	Russia claims Alaska
1850s	White whalers begin recruiting Alaskan Inuit labor
1867	Alaska becomes a U.S. Territory
1896	Klondike gold rush
1924	The Alaskan Inuit gain U.S. citizenship
1959	Alaska becomes the 49th State
1971	Native Claims Settlement Act repays the Inuit for lost land
1979	U.S. government opens Bering Sea for oil drilling

Chapter 2

Getting Around...

That's what dogsleds are for. The traditional sleds of Oogruk's past, made of driftwood, bone, or both, were the Inuit's main form of transportation on land. Basket sleds, equipped with side rails and high backs, were common in Siberia and Alaska. The sleds used in *Dogsong* are basket sleds. The rider could stand, sit, or lie on a basket sled. Dogs were hooked in pairs to a central rope called the gangline.

Chapter 2

"Milk" Blindness

Oogruk is blinded by cataracts, which have turned his dark eyes milky white. A cataract is a thickening of the cornea, or lens of the eye. Cataract victims can sometimes make out light, blurry forms, or colors. As recently as 20 years ago, cataracts meant permanent vision loss. In many cases today, it takes mere minutes for a surgeon to remove the thickened cornea and replace it with a plastic lens, restoring clear vision.

Chapter 3

From Mukluks to Muktuk

In the old days, Inuit life revolved around hunting whales, seals, and caribou. These animals provided food and much more. In the treeless Arctic, whale ribs became frameworks for houses, boats, tents, and sleds. Seal and caribou skins became boat hulls and tent coverings, bedding and clothing. Mukluks, soft, high boots, were pieced from sealskin, stuffed with grass for insulation. Muktuk, a treat high in vitamin C, was made from small cubes of raw, fatty whaleskin, eaten fresh or cured in aged seal oil.

Seal of Approval

At Arctic temperatures, seawater freezes into thick plates that stretch for miles offshore. Inuit men and boys trek for days over this sea ice on annual seal and whale hunts. Near the open sea, wind heaps the ice into long mounds of pale-turquoise slabs. Hunters climb these mounds to scout for prey. In some Alaskan villages, when a boy kills his first seal, his mother throws a huge party. She gives part of the seal, as well as other food and gifts, to every family in the community.

VOCABULARY Chapters 2, 3 **Inuit Technology**		
	umiak	skin boat built to hold several people
	harpoon	spear with a line tied to it, used for hunting whales or seals
	sinew	stringlike material made of animal tendon
	toggle	hinged connector
	stanchion	upright post
	runnershoes	hard material covering the bottoms of sled runners

No Word for Whoa!

Many beginning drivers, including Russel, learn the hard way that there is no command to stop the dogs. Sled dogs aren't taught to pull; they do it naturally from the age of six or nine months. They're often so eager to be off that drivers don't need a command to start them. Lead dogs are trained to turn right when they hear the word "Gee" and left when they hear "Haw." Most dogsleds have friction brakes and carry a snowhook, like a small anchor, that the driver must throw and set in order to stop.

Chapter 6

Sky Show

Above Russel, the Northern Lights shimmer. Astronomers think this sky show is caused by charged solar particles, swirling in the magnetic fields above Earth's poles. (A similar display, the Southern Lights, appears over Antarctica.)

Ptarmi—What?

Arctic animals are unique. Ptarmigan (tär'mǐ-gən), game birds the size of chickens, live in the freezing Arctic year round. Caribou, which look like reindeer, are furred with special, hollow hairs to hold warmth. They migrate seasonally in search of food, and the Inuit traditionally tracked the herds. Lemmings, or Arctic mice, periodically migrate, too, in scurrying swarms, though no one knows why. The Inuit still enjoy eating all these animals and more, including foxes, weasels, and musk oxen.

Chapter 7

Mammoth Moves

In Russel's dream, an Ice-Age Inuit hunter confronts a woolly mammoth. Could this really have happened? Well, yes. Cave paintings and fossils show that woolly mammoths—closely related to today's elephants and extinct for 10,000 years—evolved in Europe. They migrated to North America around 50,000 years ago—right in the middle of the last Ice Age. Frozen woolly mammoths, dating from that time, have been found in Alaskan glaciers. Ice-Age Inuit burial sites have yielded lances like the one in Russel's dream, with toggle points made to detach and hook into the prey.

Short Cut?

So how did woolly mammoths from Europe cross the ocean to North America? They walked. During the last Ice Age, which began 150,000 years ago and ended 10,000 years ago, so much sea water froze that ocean levels dropped. Land appeared, icy but firm, between Siberia and Alaska. animals crossed the "bridge." Alaska's first people did as well.

Team Players

Scientists think that Inuit village dogs, like those in Oogruk's team, evolved from tamed wolves. Short-faced Ice-Age wolves, whose fossils have been found in Alaska, may have looked much like the "great, gray" dogs in Russel's dream. However, dog breeders today report bad luck when they cross wolves with Alaskan huskies. Huskies get along well in teams, but wolves struggle to dominate. Husky-wolf hybrids are powerful, but they're too busy fighting their teammates to pull.

Coming of Age

Most cultures around the world view growing up as a major life event. Once young people in these cultures approach adulthood, they participate in public rituals or ceremonies called *rites of passage.* A rite of passage ceremony recognizes or celebrates a young person's coming of age, and the new roles and responsibilities that come with it. Here are a few examples.

- When a Jewish boy or girl turn 13 (12 in Israel), he or she accepts responsibility for following the Commandments in a ceremony called a **Bar Mitzvah** (for boys) or a **Bas** or **Bat Mitzvah** (for girls).

- Christian young people celebrate their passage into spiritual adulthood in the sacrament of **Confirmation.**

- Native American cultures (and cultures with similar beliefs, like Russel's) have a ritual called a **vision quest,** in which a young boy travels to an isolated location to make contact with the Guardian Spirit who will guide him throughout the rest of his life. There are many forms of vision quests, some that allow female participants, and some that have been embraced by other cultures.

Chapter 11
The Spirit World

Traditional Inuit beliefs hold that every person, animal, and force of nature has a spirit. When a person or animal dies, the spirit goes to live in the spirit world. People often left tools and clothing with the dead to use in the afterlife.

Chapter 14
Dressed for Success

Polar bears are well-suited—literally—for their chilly home. The hairs in their fur "suits" are hollow, trapping air for thermal warmth. Their white coloring lets them blend in with the snow when sneaking up on their dinner. (Those black noses give them away, though, so when lying in wait for seals, their main prey, they cover their noses with their paws.) In the 1960s, polar bears had been hunted almost to extinction. Today, thanks to an international treaty protecting them, their population has rebounded to nearly 40,000.

FOR YOUR INFORMATION · FYI · FOR YOUR INFORMATION

"Susan Butcher" from Champions

BY BILL LITTLEFIELD

Pause for Paws

Over the years, the annual Iditarod race has earned increasing criticism because of dog deaths. Causes of death range from moose attacks to exhaustion. Thanks, in part, to Susan Butcher's efforts in the 1980s, the Iditarod now requires better dog care, and veterinarians wait at each checkpoint to monitor the dogs' condition. Drivers must pay attention to everything from nutrition to paw inspections— and with good reason. During the Iditarod, each foot of a dog may touch the ground 1.3 million times.

"The High One"

It's the highest point in North America—and Susan Butcher climbed it with a dog team. Soaring up from the Alaskan interior, Mt. McKinley was formed before the most recent Ice Age. Its sheer shape was then sculpted by Ice-Age glaciers. Native Americans called the peak Denali, meaning "the high one." The mountain's South Peak is 20,320 feet high (the North Peak measures 19,470 feet). In the late 1800s, the U.S. Congress renamed it Mt. McKinley, after the politician who would later become the 25th President of the United States. In 1917 Mt. McKinley and its surrounding area were designated as Denali National Park, and today the mountain is known as Denali/Mt. McKinley.

Honest Dogs

The Alaskan husky, used by Susan Butcher and most other Iditarod racers, is not an official breed. To come up with these amazing dogs, breeders have crossed assorted Inuit village dogs (themselves of mixed ancestry), Alaskan malamutes, Siberian huskies, Irish setters, and even hounds. Alaskan huskies can reach speeds of 22 miles per hour and maintain them for sprints of 20 or 30 miles. Their cruising speed is 10 to 15 miles per hour. They are known as "honest dogs" because they seem to run for the joy of it and seldom do less than their best.

Race for Life

The Iditarod race roughly parallels the course of a different race—a race against illness—that took place in Alaska in 1925. An outbreak of the disease diphtheria had begun in Nome, and the only available serum was in Anchorage. The serum was loaded onto a train, but the train was stopped by impassable snowdrifts at Nenana, still 700 miles from Nome. A group of dogsledders organized a relay to bring the serum the rest of the way. Twenty-one teams participated, completing the run in only 5½ days. Kaltag, Shaktolik, and other villages that served as stops on the relay also serve as checkpoints on the Iditarod today.

VOCABULARY		
Meeting Challenges	conviction	a strong belief
	musher	a person who drives a dogsled
	mettle	courage
	crevasse	a deep, wide crack in a glacier
	domain	kingdom

The King of Mazy May

BY JACK LONDON

Background

American author Jack London (1876–1916) had a brief but extraordinary life. At age 17 he went off to sea, hunting seals in Hawaii, Japan, and Siberia. He was just over 20 when he joined the Klondike gold rush. His first book (an adventure story—what else?) came out when he was 24, igniting his career as a highly acclaimed author. London felt deep compassion for the poor, the ill, and the aged, as "The King of Mazy May" shows. He devoted himself to writing, political activism, and adventure—often all at once—until his death at age 40.

Yukon Gold

It was 1896 when four prospectors found a bonanza of gold in Canada's Yukon. Soon people were flocking to the Klondike River Valley to prospect. In a two-year period, over 100,000 hopefuls set out for Canada and Alaska, where the Yukon River became a source of more rich gold strikes. Dawson, in eastern Alaska, became a boom town. From Dawson prospecters set out in carts and sleds pulled by everything from dogs to turkeys, and to Dawson, if they were lucky, they returned to record their claims.

VOCABULARY

Do You Speak Gold Rush?

The miners of the Klondike gold rush often used these words.

prospect	to search for gold or other valuable minerals
claim	a piece of land marked out by a miner as his own
jump	to steal a claim
stampeder	person who tries to take advantage of new gold strikes
shaft	the entrance tunnel to a mine
mush	command to start sled dogs running
steel-shod	having runners coated with steel

Quartz Clues

Walt's father is off prospecting for quartz because gold veins often run through deposits of this crystalline mineral. Quartz, sparkly and harder than glass, is a semiprecious stone used in jewelry. White quartz chunks are easy to spot in a streambed or on a hillside. So, to a miner, a piece of quartz is like an arrow that reads, "Dig For Gold Here!"

Mush!

What Yukon prospectors needed most—more than picks, shovels, beans, or bandannas—were dogs. With a dogsled and good dogs, almost anything was possible. Without them, as Loren Hall's experiences show, a person was in trouble. The Yukon gold rush brought new breeds to work alongside the malamutes, huskies, and samoyeds traditionally used to pull sleds. Profiteers shipped boatloads of dogs—many of them stolen—to Alaska. Setters and collies, spaniels and bull terriers, St. Bernards, airedales, and German Shepherds were some of the breeds tried. Those that survived interbred later with the standard sled dogs.

A Mother's Yarn

RETOLD BY JAMES RIORDAN

Background

Lapland isn't a country. It's a cultural region stretching across the northern tips of Norway, Sweden, and Finland into northwestern Russia. Parts of it are forested with stunted trees, mainly firs and dwarf birch, but much of the area lies beyond where trees grow, north of the Arctic Circle. There, among rounded stones and shallow lakes, reindeer graze on the short tundra grasses and nibble "reindeer moss," a greyish lichen.

Reindeer Herders of the Far North

The people of Lapland, called Lapps or Sami, have traditionally lived by herding reindeer. They supplemented their main diet of reindeer milk and meat by hunting and fishing. They used reindeer-pulled sleds in the same way that the Inuit used dogsleds. Today's Lapps live in fishing or farming villages.

Mystery History

The Lapps speak a language related to Finnish, Hungarian, and Turkish. Anthropologists think the members of this group all lived together, thousands of years ago, near the Black Sea. At some point, for reasons that remain a mystery, they separated and migrated to various parts of Europe and Asia. No one knows why the Lapps settled in the harsh Arctic.

LITERARY CONCEPT
The Oral Tradition

"A Mother's Yarn" is an example of literature from the oral tradition. Tales like this one have been passed down orally for generations, with children hearing them from parents and reciting them to their own children. When "A Mother's Yarn" was told long ago, listeners didn't just sit there. They acted out the parts and recited favorite lines along with the storyteller. Everyone probably chimed in on the repeated line "Nastai, remember what I taught you." Listeners would also cheer heroes and denounce villains. As you read, imagine how the listeners might respond to the end of the tale.

VOCABULARY

Foods of Lapland

cloudberry	a berry similar to the raspberry but paler and smaller
venison	deer meat
rusk	a piece of stale bread dipped in milk and toasted until crisp
partridge	a European game bird related to quails and pheasants

Glossary

Section 1: Chapters 1–5

abrupt* (ə-brŭpt′): *adj.* sudden and unexpected *p. 45*

aloof* (ə-lōōf′): *adj.* reserved; standoffish *p. 12*

cache (kăsh): *n.* hidden supply of food or other goods *p. 8*

carcass (kär′kəs): *n.* body of a dead animal *p. 39*

diminish* (dĭ-mĭn′ĭsh): *v.* to become less *p. 44*

ferment (fər-mĕnt′): *v.* to change because of the growth of bacteria or mold *p. 18*

grimace* (grĭm′ĭs): *v.* to twist the face into an unusual expression *p. 13*

gutter (gŭt′ər): *v.* to burn low and flicker *p. 15*

laminated (lăm′ə-nā′tĭd): *adj.* pressed together in layers *p. 22*

lunge (lŭnj): *v.* to make a sudden forward movement *p. 40*

opaque* (ō-pāk′): *adj.* not letting light through *p. 14*

rancid (răn′sĭd): *adj.* stale *p. 18*

rebuke* (rĭ-byōōk′): *n.* scolding *p. 34*

supple* (sŭp′əl): *adj.* flexing or moving easily *p. 23*

tundra (tŭn′drə): *n.* a treeless arctic plain with frost beneath the surface year round *p. 7*

wince* (wĭns): *v.* to flinch or recoil in pain *p. 8*

wraith (rāth): *n.* ghostly form *p. 50*

Section 2: Chapters 6–10

audible* (ô′də-bəl): *adj.* able to be heard *p. 73*

destination* (dĕs′tə-nā′shən): *n.* arrival place; goal *p. 91*

exultation* (ĕg′zŭl-tā′shən): *n.* great joy; triumph *p. 76*

forlorn* (fôr-lôrn′): *adj.* deserted; sad *p. 64*

glaze (glāz): *v.* to become glassy *p. 69*

immense* (ĭ-mĕns′): *adj.* very large *p. 74*

interval (ĭn′tər-vəl): *n.* the amount of time between two specified periods *p. 83*

plight* (plīt): *n.* bad or dangerous situation *p. 87*

proclaim* (prō-klām′): *v.* to announce *p. 87*

ravenous* (răv′ən-əs): *adj.* very hungry *p. 89*

render (rĕn′dər): *v.* to turn clear and crisp from heating *p. 83*

PRONUNCIATION KEY

ă	at, gas	îr	dear, here	th	thing, with
ā	ape, day	ng	sing, anger	*th*	then, other
ä	father, barn	ŏ	odd, not	ŭ	up, nut
âr	fair, dare	ō	open, road, grow	ûr	fur, earn, bird, worm
ĕ	egg, ten	ô	awful, bought, horse	zh	treasure, garage
ē	evil, see, meal	oi	coin, boy	ə	awake, even, pencil,
hw	white, everywhere	ŏŏ	look, full		pilot, focus
ĭ	inch, fit	ōō	root, glue, through	ər	perform, letter
ī	idle, my, tried	ou	out, cow		

Sounds in Foreign Words

kh	*German* ich, auch; *Scottish* loch	œ	*French* feu, cœur; *German* schön	ü	*French* utile, rue; *German* grün
n	*French* entre, bon, fin				

* The words followed by asterisks are useful words that you might add to your vocabulary.

Glossary (continued)

Section 3: Chapters 11–15

agony (ăg'ə-nē): *n.* great physical or emotional pain *p. 105*

bleak* (blēk): *adj.* exposed to the elements; cold; sad *p. 106*

cease* (sēs): *v.* to stop *p. 104*

gut (gŭt): *v.* to remove the internal organs *p. 97*

indication (ĭn-dĭ-kā'shən): *n.* sign or gesture *p. 103*

impertinent (ĭm-pûrt'n-ənt): *adj.* rude or disrespectful *p. 112*

liberally* (lĭb'ər-ə-lē): *adv.* freely and generously *p. 122*

pummel (pŭm'əl): *v.* to hit repeatedly *p. 120*

reluctantly* (rĭ-lŭk'tənt-lē): *adv.* in an unwilling way *p. 122*

revive* (rĭ-vīv'): *v.* to return to life *p. 123*

strangulation (străng'gyə-lā'shən): *n.* death by squeezing the throat to stop the breath *p. 97*

submission (səb-mĭish'ən): *n.* giving in to a greater power or authority *p. 101*

vanish* (văn'ĭsh): *v.* to disappear *p. 114*

* The words followed by asterisks are useful words that you might add to your vocabulary.

Name _____

Solving Problems

Russel faces several problems in this section. He has help in solving some problems and he solves others on his own. Fill in the chart below by describing either a problem or a solution. Identify anyone who helps Russel to solve a problem. The first one is done for you.

Problem	Solution
Chapter 1 • Russel is unhappy and isn't quite sure why. • Russel's father wants help for Russel.	• Russel talks to his father. • Russel's father sends Russel to Oogruk.
Chapter 2 • Russel wants to become more than he is.	• _____ _____
Chapter 3 • Russel tries to hunt birds but his arrows keep missing.	• _____ _____
Chapter 4 • _____ _____ • A blizzard comes up too fast for Russel and the dogs to outrun it.	• Russel growls at Oogruk's lead dog and bites its snout. • Russel lets the lead dog choose its own direction.
Chapter 5 • Oogruk dies just as Russel begins his journey.	• Russel harpoons an ice floe to use as a bridge.

Understanding Chronological Order

Events in *Dogsong* occur in chronological or time order. Some events take place while Russel is awake, and others take place in his dreams. As you read, fill in the chart below to keep track of both kinds of events.

While Russel Is Awake

While Russel Dreams

Chapter 6: Russel kills four caribou, getting food and shelter for himself and the dogs.

Chapter 7:

Chapter 8:

Chapter 9: Russel "sees" the hunter visit an unfamiliar settlement and share his songs.

Chapter 10:

Name _____

Drawing Conclusions from Details

Thinking about the details from Russel's dreams and from his waking life can help you draw conclusions about Russel. Locate details in this section to complete each sentence below. Then "add up" each set of details to make a general statement about Russel.

	Details about Russel's sense of responsibility
+	Chapter 12: When a storm comes up as Russel follows footprints from a snowmobile, he decides to _____
+	Chapter 14: When Russel has been away from Nancy for six days and finds no game, he decides to _____
+	Chapter 14: When Russel realizes that Nancy needs a doctor, he decides to _____
=	**General statement:** _____

	Details about Russel's attitude toward his dreams
+	Chapter 12: When Russel wants to see if Nancy is alive, he imitates his dream by _____
+	Chapter 14: When Russel must kill the polar bear, he imitates his dream by _____
+	Chapter 14: After Russel has meat, he goes back to Nancy immediately because _____
=	**General statement:** _____

Literary Concept ①

PLOT

The series of events in a story is called the plot. In a typical plot, story events can be grouped under three major parts:

- The exposition introduces the characters and reveals any conflicts.
- The climax is the turning point, usually one event that is the most exciting of the story.
- The resolution is made up of events that follow the climax and end the story.

Depending on how a story unfolds, the number of events that can be grouped under each major part might vary. As you read *Dogsong*, answer the questions below about the events. Be prepared to defend your answers and your description of the climax in a discussion with your classmates.

Exposition of *Dogsong*

Why is Russel unhappy with himself? _____
_____

How does Oogruk help Russel to find himself? _____
_____

How do Oogruk's dogs change as Russel deals with them? _____
_____

Why does Russel sense he has a connection to the people in his dreams?
_____
_____

Why does Nancy want to stay with Russel? _____
_____

Climax of *Dogsong*

What is the climax of *Dogsong*? _____
_____

Resolution of *Dogsong*

Why does Russel race back to Nancy with the meat? _____
_____

What important events does Russel mention in his song?
_____
_____

Literary Concept 2

MOOD

The mood of a story is the feeling it gives readers. In *Dogsong*, as in most novels, the mood changes many times as the story unfolds. Gary Paulsen uses details of setting—the time and place of the action—to help create the varying moods in *Dogsong*.

For each event in the chart below, list details of setting. (The first one is done for you.) The write a word or phrase that sums up the mood, or main feeling you pick up, at that point in the novel.

Event	Details about the setting	Mood
Russel takes his first dogsled run.	Place: out on the sea ice Weather: cold, windy Kind of light: daylight	
Oogruk dies.	Place: Weather: Kind of light:	
Russel finds the lamp.	Place: Weather: Kind of light:	
Russel finds Nancy.	Place: Weather: Kind of light:	
Russel and Nancy return to civilization.	Place: Weather: Kind of light:	

Gary Paulsen uses **figurative language** to say things in original ways. Figurative language often takes one of these three forms:

- A **simile** is a comparison using the word like or as.

- A **metaphor** is a comparison of two things that simply states that one thing is another, using forms of the verb to be.

- **Personification** is a description in which a human characteristics are given to an animal, object, or an idea.

Read the examples of figurative language from *Dogsong*. In the spaces, write the kind of comparison that each example represents: simile, metaphor, or personification. One is done for you.

_____ 1. ". . . the sounds . . . grated like the ends of a broken bone."

_____ 2. ". . . the voice moved like strong music."

_____ 3. "The dogs were his eyes."

_____ 4. "'. . . gone . . . Like melted ice in the spring.'"

_____ 5. ". . . the land fought to hold the snow."

_____ 6. ". . . the dogs looked like jewels. . . "

___personification___ 7. ". . . the northern lights would come to dance."

_____ 8. ". . . the dogs were . . . fog that had come alive."

_____ 9. "His legs are the earth. . . ."

_____ 10. "She spoke in a whisper that was almost a hiss."

_____ 11. ". . . the wind slashes and looks for their lives. The hungry wind."

_____ 12. ". . . the snow machine. . . was sitting on its skis, just squatting. . ."

Name _____

A. The words on the left column appear with asterisks in the Glossary on pages 31–32. Draw a line to connect each word from the left column with its antonym (the word most nearly opposite in meaning) on the right.

1. abrupt   begin

2. cease   tiny

3. supple   transparent

4. opaque   stiff

5. immense   gradual

B. The underlined words below appear with asterisks in the Glossary. For each sentence, write **Y** if the underlined word is used in a way that fits its meaning. Write **N** if the word is used in a way that doesn't fit its meaning.

_____ **1.** When the dogs finally stopped, they were too <u>ravenous</u> to eat a thing.

_____ **2.** On reaching the coast, Russel and Nancy smiled in <u>exultation.</u>

_____ **3.** The lead dog whined, but the sound was so <u>audible</u> that Russel didn't hear it.

_____ **4.** Russel gave the dogs a <u>rebuke</u> whenever he was happy with them.

_____ **5.** Russel took off his outer parka as the cold began to <u>diminish.</u>

C. Use the clues to fill in the crossword puzzle with asterisked words from the Glossary.

Across

1. a bad situation

2. deserted

3. to make a face

Down

1. to announce

2. to return to life

Beyond the Literature

Culminating Writing Assignments

EXPLORATORY WRITING

1. Time has gone by and Russel Susskit has grown older, but he has never forgotten all that Oogruk gave him. Now his teenage children want to know about the people who shaped his life. Write Russel's **memoir** of Oogruk. Choose specifics to show how Oogruk looked and acted and what his importance was to Russel.

2. *Dogsong* ends as Russel and Nancy approach a village. What happens afterwards? Write one or more **scenes** showing Russel and Nancy one year after the close of the novel. Show where they are, how each is living, what they are doing, and what place (if any) they have in each other's lives.

3. *Dogsong* is narrated from Russel's point of view. How might other characters' points of view be different? Choose one event in the novel, and retell it in a **monologue.** Use the point of view of a character who participated: Russel's father, Oogruk, the Ice Age man or woman, or Nancy.

RESEARCH

1. Russel is astonished to see a polar bear, knowing that they are near extinction. Learn more about polar bears and other endangered Arctic animals, and about what is being done to protect them. In a **letter to the editor,** present your opinions on the efforts to protect these animals. Use information from your research to support your points.

2. Oogruk's dogs aren't pets—they're working dogs. Research other kinds of working dogs. Present a **report** on the training, jobs, and accomplishments of these animals.

3. Examine other "dangerous journey" stories in mythology (such as *Jason and the Argonauts*), fantasy (such as *A Wrinkle in Time* or *The Hobbit*), or contemporary fiction or nonfiction (such as *A Boat to Nowhere* or *Survive the Savage Seas.*) Write a **comparison** of the journey in one of these literary works and Russel's journey in *Dogsong*.

LITERARY ANALYSIS

1. Russel's long dogsled trip is a quest—a journey in search of a treasure. He returns with a stone lamp, part of a polar bear hide, and a companion. In an **essay,** explain how each of these is a treasure for Russel. Use details from *Dogsong* to illustrate your points.

2. **Character Analysis:** Oogruk calls Russel a "true person." How do you think Oogruk would define "true person"? State the **definition** in your own words, and show how Russel fits the definition.

3. Do you agree with critic Georgia Johnson that the rituals and the vision quest in *Dogsong* make the novel hard to understand? Present your ideas in a **review** of *Dogsong*. Support your opinions with specifics from the novel and from your own experience.

*For writing instruction in specific modes, have students use the **Writing Coach.**

40 Literature Connections

Multimodal Activities

Let It Shine

It's just a small stone bowl, but the ancient Eskimo lamp has many levels of importance for Russel. Invite students to use magazine clippings, "found objects," and their own artwork to create **collages** expressing the significance of the lamp.

Words of Wisdom

"You don't get songs," explains Oogruk. "You *are* a song." What other thought-provoking sayings do *Dogsong* and the related readings offer? Have students work in groups to copy memorable quotations from the readings and create an illustration for each quotation. They might mount the illustrations and quotations as a **bulletin board display** or bind them into an **anthology.**

Child's Play

Challenge students to use ideas from the novel to design a **game** that could be played in a small Arctic shelter while waiting out a storm. They might put a new spin on a familiar game, perhaps creating a version of "Stone, Paper, Scissors" that reflects the tools and weapons Russel and Oogruk use. Or they might research actual Eskimo games for ideas. Have them write up their game rules, including helpful illustrations, and make prototypes of any necessary equipment.

Captured Moments

Engage students in compiling **photo essays** to chronicle contemporary coming-of-age rituals that have meaning for them. Each photo essay should include captions and a brief explanatory text, perhaps with quotations from participants. The explanatory text might compare the events in the photos to events from Russel's trek in *Dogsong*.

Let's Hear It

Suggest that interested students set Russel's song to music. Have them work in groups to make an **audiotape** featuring their scores and Russel's words. They might compose and play their own music—anything from a simple drumbeat to a more complex arrangement. Or they might choose existing instrumental music to provide an appropriate background for a reading of Russel's song.

Cross-Curricular Projects

Try It; You'll Like It

"Hire" students as advertising executives. Tell them their client is a trek outfitter who sells supplies to groups planning Arctic expeditions. The students' job is to create **TV commercials** for foods their client sells—foods such as the chipped fat, raw caribou haunch, and water-blood soup that sustain Russel, Nancy, and Oogruk. Encourage students to scan the novel for food to feature and then to make the food seem irresistible. If a video camera is available, they can tape and "air" their commercials.

Silver Screen

What if *Dogsong* were made into a movie? Let students make **movie posters** for a film version of the novel. Their posters can depict scenes that students consider especially dramatic. The posters should also include the movie title, the names of stars, and two or three phrases (such as "Thrills! Chills!") to grab viewers' interest.

Hands On

Encourage students to create **carvings, sculptures,** or **models** of people, animals, or significant items from *Dogsong*. Students can choose their subjects either from Russel's waking life or from his dreams of the Ice-Age hunter. You might provide bar soap and tools for "ivory carvings," as well as clay for sculptures and bits of wood, string, leather, and other materials for models. Have students write "Artist's Notes" to accompany their works.

And Now, the Forecast…

Engage students to script and deliver a local **TV newscast** for the events of one day in *Dogsong*. They can choose any day (including days from Russel's dreams) and can combine details from the novel with other material from their imaginations. Each newscast might also include a local weather report. Students can consult an almanac for temperatures, sun conditions, and other weather information for Arctic winters.

Picture This, Kids!

Overview:

Students will research the ways of life of modern Inuit and Yuit groups living in Siberia, Alaska, Canada, and Greenland and will use their research to create a nonfiction picture book for elementary-school children. Students' task is to work cooperatively to plan, write, illustrate, and produce their book. Their purpose is to increase younger children's understanding of the native peoples of the Arctic.

Cross-Curricular Connections: Social Studies, Sciences, Math, Art

Suggested Procedure:

1. To establish the need for this project, you might have an elementary teacher visit the class to explain that grade-school children study Native American cultures, but very little material on Eskimo cultures is available for them. Introduce the project and have students start by reading encyclopedia articles under entries such as *Inuit, Yuit,* and *Eskimo.* Based on the general information in these articles, have them list material that their book might include. They can then organize their list into a working outline. They might examine cultures by region: Siberian Yupik, Alaskan Yupik, Alaskan Inuit, Canadian Inuit, Greenland Inuit. Or they might focus on aspects of daily life: housing, food, education, arts, hunting, and so on, examining how they change from culture to culture.

2. Guide the class to consensus about the elementary grade level their book will target. Then have them examine other books intended for that grade level, to get an idea of children's interests, readability, and ratio of text to illustrations. They should modify their working outline as necessary to tailor the book to the grade level. For example, for lower grades, students might show a day in the life of a child in each of several Arctic cultures.

3. Divide students into teams; have each team choose one chapter or book section to research. Encourage them to explore the Internet and recent articles in photo-illustrated periodicals such as *National Geographic, Natural History,* and *National Wildlife,* as well as young peoples' publications such as *Cobblestone, National Geographic World,* and *Contact.* Set up a central file for their research notes.

4. Have teams write and illustrate their chapters or book sections. Then guide students in planning an overall design. They will need to decide on page count, typefaces for text and headings, treatment of illustrations, borders, and so on. They should also design a title page and possibly a glossary or an index.

5. If computers and software are available, students can use them to produce the text of their book. If no computers are available, students might choose to type their text or to use hand-lettering or calligraphy. After they have assembled the book, you might reproduce it by color photocopying. Arrange for them to share it with an elementary class, perhaps reading it aloud to the children and answering questions.

Teaching Tip

Encourage students to donate their finished book, or a copy of it, to an elementary-school library.

Northern Star

Overview:

Students will plan and present exhibits in a classroom travel fair focusing on Alaska. Students' task is to research, design, and present multimedia exhibits. The purpose of the activity is to increase awareness of the many features of America's 49th state.

Cross-Curricular Connections: Social Studies, Sciences, Math, Art, Music

Suggested Procedure:

1. You might have the class work together to generate a cluster, on the chalkboard, of images of Alaska that *Dogsong* has left them with. Ask what else they know about Alaska, and lead into a discussion of aspects of Alaska that should be investigated for a travel fair. Have students generate a list and then categorize their items under five or six major headings or topics. They might use headings such as history, geography, wilderness areas, wildlife, major cities, natural resources, people, annual events, and so on.

2. Divide students into small groups and let each group pick a topic from the list. Direct groups to research their topics. Meanwhile, set a date for the fair. If appropriate, send invitations to other classes.

3. Have groups plan creative ways to present their research. Encourage them to use more than one medium. They might combine any of the following: posters, other artwork, slides, audiotapes, live music, videos, computer presentations, hands-on demonstrations, arts and crafts workshops, geography or history bees, food sampling, models, dioramas, or exhibits of realia.

4. Help students make necessary measurements, list and obtain needed supplies, and construct their exhibits. Encourage them to rehearse their presentations.

5. On the day before the fair, teams should set up their exhibits. Have them arrange to staff the exhibits in shifts, so that everyone gets a chance to explore other presentations. On fair day, encourage students to arrive early and enjoy themselves.

Teaching Tip

This project lends itself to teaming with other teachers. Several classes might work together on a multi-state travel fair.

Suggestions for Assessment

Negotiated Rubrics

Negotiating rubrics for assessment with students allows them to know before they start an assignment what is required and how it will be judged, and gives them additional ownership of the final product. A popular method of negotiating rubrics is for the teacher and students individually to list the qualities the final product should have, then compare the teacher-generated list with the student-generated list and together decide on a compromise.

Portfolio Building

Remind students that they have many choices of types of assignments to select for their portfolios. Among these are the following:

- Culminating Writing Assignments (page 40)
- Writing Prompts, found in the Discussion Starters
- Multimodal Activities (page 41)
- Cross-Curricular Projects (pages 43–44)

Suggest that students use some of the following questions as criteria in selecting which pieces to include in their portfolios.

- Which shows my clearest thinking about the literature?
- Which is or could become most complete?
- Which shows a type of work not currently included in my portfolio?
- Which am I proudest of?

Remind students to reflect on the pieces they choose and to write a note explaining why they included each piece and how they would evaluate it.

*For suggestions about how to assess portfolios, see **Teacher's Guide to Assessment and Portfolio Use.***

Writing Assessment

The following can be made into formal assignments for evaluation:

- Culminating Writing Assignments (page 40)
- a written analysis of the Critic's Corner literary criticisms
- fully developed Writing Prompts from the Discussion Starters

*For rubrics to help you evaluate specific kinds of writing, see the **Guide to Writing Assessment** in the **Formal Assessment** booklet of **The Language of Literature.***

Test

The test on page 46–47 consists of essay and short-answer questions. The answer key follows.

Alternative Assessment

For the kinds of authentic assessments found on many state and districtwide tests, see the ***Alternative Assessment*** booklet of ***The Language of Literature.***

Test

Dogsong and Related Readings

Essay

Choose two of the following essay questions to answer on your own paper.
(25 points each)

1. How do the settings of events in the novel affect the mood? Use any three of the following events as examples: Russel's morning in his father's house; Russel's first dogsled run; Russel's close call on the sea ice; Oogruk's death; the discovery of the lamp; Russel's rescue of Nancy; the run back to the coast to get help for Nancy.

2. Explain how the dogs help Russel develop as a person. From the novel, choose three experiences that Russel has with the dogs, and decide what Russel learns or gains from each experience. Fill in the chart below with specifics about each experience. As you write your essay, use these specifics to illustrate your ideas.

Russel's experiences with the dogs	What Russel learns
_____ —>	_____
_____ —>	_____
_____ —>	_____

3. What does *Dogsong* tell you about the effects of the modern-day world on Inuit culture? List at least two effects, and show how the novel reveals these effects.

4. How do Russel's dreams of the Ice-Age people help him? Sum up the story that unfolds in his dreams. Then explain how this dream story guides Russel to rescue Nancy and to save her and himself from starvation.

5. Facing unexpected challenges can bring out a person's strengths. Examine how *Dogsong* and the related readings reflect this idea. Use examples from *Dogsong* and any two of the following readings: "The King of Mazy May," "Susan Butcher," "A Mother's Yarn," *Words on a Page*.

Short Answer

On your paper, write a short answer for each question below. Give a reason for each answer. (5 points each)

1. Why does Russel's father suggest that Russel consult Oogruk?

2. Do you agree that Oogruk's tools and weapons don't belong in a museum?

3. Why doesn't anyone in the village try to stop Russel from dropping out of school?

4. Why does Russel leave Oogruk the small harpoon before setting off on his trek?

5. How does finding the lamp change Russel's trek?

6. In Russel's dream, why do the woman and her two children die?

7. When Russel sees snowmobile tracks on his journey, what are his reasons for following them?

8. Why is Nancy unwilling to go back to her village?

9. Do you think Russel could have killed the polar bear without the dogs? Why or why not?

10. Why does Russel decide to return to civilization?

Essay

Answers to essay questions will vary, but students should state their ideas clearly and support them with details from the readings. Suggested points to look for appear below.

1. Students should demonstrate that Paulsen uses setting to reinforce mood. Russel awakens in his father's cramped house in the winter darkness, feeling spiritually cramped and bleak himself. A burst of joy comes when he makes his first run with Oogruk's dogs, out in the daylight on the broad reaches of the sea ice. His chilling brush with death on the ice comes in darkness during a freezing storm. His reassuring discovery of the lamp occurs in a cozy campsite. He finds Nancy near death in a fierce blizzard with relentless winds; and the two return to the coast in the growing light and warmth of the Arctic springtime.

2. Students might note that Russel's experiences with the dogs give him trust in his own intuition, confidence in his abilities, a new kind of respect for the animal world; leadership experience; and new strength and freedom. Possible events include the lead dog's defying Russel, when Russel learns to trust the intuitive memories from his trance with Oogruk; being stranded on the ice floe, when Russel learns to respect the dogs' instincts and to replace fear with action; tracking Nancy, when Russel imposes his will on the dogs and realizes that the lead dog is tuned to his thoughts and feelings; and the runs after he kills the polar bear, when he experiences the dogs' strength as his own and feels free.

3. Effects that students may list include alcoholism (Russel's father once had a drinking problem); illness (Russel's father has lung damage from cigarettes); changes in religion (Russel's father credits Christianity with keeping him away from alcohol and helping him solve problems. On the other hand, Christian doctrines drive Nancy to attempt suicide when she becomes pregnant, and Oogruk recalls how missionaries made people afraid and ashamed to follow their traditional religion); lifestyle changes both positive and negative (white culture has brought snowmobiles, motorboats, and guns—though these have made people forget their traditional technology and skills. It has also brought helpful medicines, doctors, and health practices such as cooking food to destroy parasites.)

4. The dream story: an Ice-Age family is thriving when the man goes off with the dogsled to hunt a woolly mammoth. After making the kill, he visits a village to sing of his hunt, but he stays too long. A storm delays his return further, and his family is left starving. The wife puts the last of the lamp oil to the children's lips. In struggling to return, the man drives his dogs too hard and kills them. The woman and children die and are eaten by animals. Without the dogs or his family, the man also dies.

How the dreams guide Russel: he tracks Nancy because the dreams make him feel that he may not be meant to stay alone; he revives Nancy by putting lamp oil to her lips; when he goes off to hunt, he leaves her with plentiful fat for the lamp; recalling the Ice-Age man's fate, he decides not to kill the dogs for food; he kills the polar bear by using the Ice-Age man's techniques; recalling the Ice-Age family's plight, he returns to Nancy as fast as possible—just in time—with the bear meat.

5. In *Dogsong*, Russel faces the challenges of attending Oogruk's death, keeping himself and the dogs alive, saving Nancy, and killing a polar bear. His experiences give him physical strength, survival skills, confidence, insights into other people, and a connection with his heritage. In "The King of Mazy May," Walt takes on the challenge of saving Loren Hall's claim and discovers his own strength, courage, and ingenuity. In "Susan Butcher," dogsled racing challenges Butcher with unexpected accidents and reversals, and she becomes increasingly resilient, philosophical, and humane. In "A Mother's Yarn," the unexpected loss of both parents challenges Nastai, and she becomes self-sufficient, creative, and gracious. In "Words on a Page," Lenore is challenged by the unexpected conflict between her desire to become a writer and her desire to stay close to her father; she develops new communications skills, deepened compassion, and a firmer sense of purpose.

Short Answer

On your paper, write a short answer for each question below. Give a reason for each answer. (5 points each)

1. Mr. Susskit knows that Russel is unhappy, that he himself can't help his son, and that Oogruk, grounded in the old ways, has deep wisdom.

2. Answers will vary, but students should note Oogruk's point that his tools and weapons are practical items that have a place in daily life, not relics to be displayed. He wants to keep them maintained and ready for use, not to retire them into a glass case.

3. Everyone in the village knows that Russel is learning from Oogruk what he most needs to learn. They consider Russel competent to decide his own direction, and by Eskimo standards, interfering would be rude.

4. He wants Oogruk to have the harpoon to hunt for seals in the afterlife, so he leaves it with Oogruk's body on the ice. Russel is following the old ways and finding that traditional Eskimo beliefs about the afterlife feel right to him.

5. It gives Russel an efficient, reliable source of warmth and light—requiring no wood, a boon in the treeless arctic—and an easy way to heat food. It also buoys his morale. Its age and elegant, hand-worked design make it beautiful to him, and he considers it a sign that his quest is on the right track.

6. They die of starvation and cold when the man fails to return in time with food. They are forced to eat their clothing, and they run out of fat for the lamp. The man is delayed by his own irresponsibility. He lets his dogs lead him into a village, stays to enjoy himself, and then meets an unexpected storm.

7. He hopes the person on the snowmobile will have a pot he can use to melt snow in. Besides, the dogs follow the tracks, and Russel is beginning to feel that the dogs respond to his unconscious desires. He thinks one message from his dreams may be that he doesn't want to be alone forever.

8. She becomes pregnant and the missionaries in her village convince her that her pregnancy is sinful because she is unmarried. She doesn't feel connected to anyone there, where no one has dogs anymore and the old ways have apparently died out. She understands Russel, is comfortable with him, and wants to stay with him.

9. Answers will vary, but students should note that one dog attacks the bear and distracts it, causing it to turn slightly as it charges Russel, so that he can guide the lance directly toward its heart.

10. Nancy doesn't recover after the premature stillbirth. Russel realizes that she needs medical help quickly, and he is determined to get it for her. He cares about her.

Other Works by Gary Paulsen

Dancing Carl. 1983.
Through the winter, a strange man in a worn flight jacket dances on the ice of a skating area, and the inexpressible begins to find expression. ALA Best Books for Young Adults.

Tracker. 1984.
Thirteen-year-old John, facing a hunting season alone for the first time because of his grandfather's illness, comes to a deepened understanding of life and death. ALA Best Books for Young Adults.

Sentries. 1986.
Concern about nuclear disaster connects the lives of four young people, who consider themselves misfits, with the lives of three veterans of past wars.

Hatchet. 1987.
A hatchet takes on new meaning for a boy stranded in the Alaskan wilderness after a plane crash. A Newbery Honor Book.

The Island. 1988.
A boy finds his strengths and his values after spending a summer by himself on an Alaskan island offshore from his parents' home.

The Madonna Stories. 1988.
A collection of short stories about women whose toughness and compassion shine through their daily lives.

The Winter Room. 1987.
Through the voice of a young narrator, Paulsen evokes the splendors of seasonal changes and celebrates family life, farm life, and the art of storytelling. A Newbery Honor Book.

Woodsong. 1990.
Paulsen recounts his experiences as an outdoorsman, including the story of the unforgettable dog Storm and a journal-like account of running the Iditarod. Nonfiction.

Winterdance. 1994.
A detailed recollection of Paulsen's involvement in the Iditarod: the years spent training, the trek to Alaska, the course of the race, and Paulsen's observations and challenges, successes and failures during the two-week race itself. Nonfiction.

FICTION

George, Jean Craighead. *Julie of the Wolves.* New York: Harper & Row, 1972. A troubled Eskimo girl runs away to live on her own in the wilderness, where she forges a relationship with a wolf pack. Newbery Medal. **(easy)**

Hemingway, Ernest. *The Old Man and the Sea.* New York: Charles Scribner's Sons, 1952. Alone in his skiff far out at sea, a peasant fisherman calls on a lifetime of experience and insights as he fights to bring in a giant marlin. **(average)**

Houston, James. *Akavak: An Inuit-Eskimo Legend.* New York: Harcourt Brace Jovanovich, 1968. The "impossible" dogsled journey of a heroic Canadian Inuit boy and his equally heroic grandfather. **(easy)**

Mohr, Nicholasa. *Going Home.* New York: Dial, 1986. On a trip to Puerto Rico, Felita bridges the gulf between her New York upbringing and her Puerto Rican heritage. **(average)**

O'Dell, Scott. *Island of the Blue Dolphins.* New York: Dell, 1978. Historical fiction: a Native American girl, left alone on an unpopulated island, lives on her own for eighteen years before being found. Newbery Medal. **(average)**

Rawls, Wilson. *Where the Red Fern Grows.* New York: Doubleday: 1961. An Ozarks boy comes of age during his years with the coonhounds he raises and loves. **(average)**

Walter, Mildred Pitts. *The Girl on the Outside.* New York: Scholastic, 1982. Historical fiction: Eva finds her own ways to triumph over harrowing ordeals as the first African-American at a Little Rock, Arkansas, high school. **(challenge)**

NONFICTION

Casey, Brigid, and Wendy Haugh. *Sled Dogs.* New York: Dodd, Mead & Company, 1983. Sled dog behavior, dogsled technique, and the history of dogsledding. Illustrated with photographs, old prints, and drawings. **(average)**

Frank, Anne. *The Diary of Anne Frank.* New York: Random House, 1956. The daily life, and the inner journey, of a girl forced into two years of hiding when Nazis invade her home during World War II. **(average)**

Graham, Robin Lee. *The Boy Who Sailed Around the World Alone.* New York: Golden Press, 1973. In this journal, 16-year-old Robin records the terrors and triumphs of his solitary voyage aboard his small sloop, the Dove. **(average)**

Kroeber, Theodora. *Ishi, Last of His Tribe.* Bantam, 1973. Biography of the courageous last survivor of the "lost" Yahi tribe, who found ways to maintain his values and preserve his culture. **(average)**

Matthiessen, Peter. *The Snow Leopard.* New York: Penguin, 1987. Matthiessen treks through the icy Himalayas of Nepal, glimpsing the rare snow leopard, on a quest for wisdom and inner peace. **(challenge)**

Mowat, Farley. *Never Cry Wolf.* New York: Bantam, 1983. A naturalist with a sense of humor records his experiences while observing a wolf pack in the Canadian Arctic, aided by an Eskimo family. **(challenge)**

Niehardt, John G. *Black Elk Speaks.* New York: Pocket Books, 1972. A holy man of the Lakota Sioux shares his visions and his songs. **(challenge)**

Ring, Elizabeth. *Sled Dogs: Arctic Athletes.* Brookfield, Conn.: Millbrook Press, 1994. Sled dog characteristics and breeds, as well as information about dogsleds. **(easy)**

Wadsworth, Ginger. *Susan Butcher: Sled Dog Racer.* Minneapolis: Lerner Publications, 1994. A biography of Susan Butcher (1956–), multiple winner of the Iditarod. Includes photos, maps, and statistics. **(easy)**

MULTIMEDIA

Dogsong. Sound recording and filmstrip. Random House/Miller-Brody, 1986. **(audiocassette and filmstrip)**

The Call of the Wild. Video recording. MPI Home Video, 1972. 105 min. Starring Charlton Heston. Buck, a pet dog, comes into his own after he is stolen and shipped to the Klondike to pull dogsleds during the gold rush of 1896. **(videocassette)**

Never Cry Wolf. Video Recording. Walt Disney Home Video, 1993. 105 min. Arctic adventure, based on the book by Farley Mowat. **(videocassette)**